HELLO DEAR

PREVIOUS BOOKS BY HUBERT MOORE

Down by a Bicycle, Hippopotamus Press, 1979
Namesakes, Enitharmon Press, 1988
Rolling Stock, Enitharmon Press, 1991
Left-Handers, Enitharmon Press, 1995
Touching Down in Utopia, Shoestring Press, 2002
The Hearing Room, Shoestring Press, 2006
Whistling Back, Shoestring Press, 2012
The Bright Gaze of the Disoriented, Shoestring Press, 2014
The Tree Line, Shoestring Press, 2017
The Feeding Station, Shoestring Press, 2019
Owl Songs, Shoestring Press, 2019
Country of Arrival, Shoestring Press, 2022

HELLO DEAR

59 new poems

HUBERT MOORE

All rights reserved. No part of this work covered by the copyright herein may be reproduced or used in any means – graphic, electronic, or mechanical, including copying, recording, taping, or information storage and retrieval systems – without written permission of the publisher.

Printed by imprintdigital
Upton Pyne, Exeter
www.digital.imprint.co.uk

Typesetting and cover design by The Book Typesetters
hello@thebooktypesetters.com
07422 598 168
www.thebooktypesetters.com

Published by Shoestring Press
19 Devonshire Avenue, Beeston, Nottingham, NG9 1BS
(0115) 925 1827
www.shoestringpress.co.uk

First published 2023
© Copyright: Hubert Moore
© Cover painting: Haymanot Tesfa
© Photograph of author: Darrie Payne

The moral right of the author has been asserted.

ISBN 978-1-915553-23-2

ACKNOWLEDGEMENTS

Thanks and admiration to Haymanot Tesfa for her painting on the front cover. Many thanks to Darrie Payne for his photograph of the author.

Also to Ambrose Musiyiwa for inclusion of *Collisions* in his new collection, *Welcome to Britain* (Civic Leicester). Also to the editor of *Scintilla* for publishing *The Red Kite* and *Believing in Eagles*.

This collection is dedicated to people who reject hostility, welcomers everywhere.

CONTENTS

Hello dear	1
In the tilth	2
Raining up	3
Clips	4
Bike ride	5
Long slow fall	6
Joins	7
Grey gold	8
Sir	9
Children crossing	10
Double-ended saw	11
The other half	12
Dawdling	13
The slow movement	14
Believing in eagles	15
Red kite	16
Floods came	17
Salvia	18
Arrangement with water	19
Half-arranging	20
Why would the road?	21
Mountain Street	22
Sitting by Isledon Road	23
Pencilling over	24
Balancing act	25
At the artist's house	26
Waiting for Wayne	27
In gas	28
Weather and news	29
In the queue	30
Parallel lines	31
Rain on the window	32
The wisdom of Eli	33

For Haymanot	34
Lime-grief	35
In the kitchen	36
Love note	37
How the eyes smile	38
Somewhere between	39
Shunt	40
Drill	41
Enid's ladder	42
Butcher's name	43
Collisions	44
Humanity	45
Humans	46
A thread of cotton	47
Survivor	48
No talking before breakfast	49
Acequia	50
Tomato-growing	51
Man outside	52
Bedtime story	53
Hospital	54
Moon poem	55
Worming in	56
A and E	57
Unfixed abode	58
No fear	59

HELLO DEAR

The title refers to the greeting in a message written by a girl detained, amongst other refugees, at Manston Processing Centre in Kent in autumn 2022. She threw her letter, pleading for help, over the fence in a bottle. Learn more here:

Hello dear. The message
in the bottle, addressed to
*Journalists, Organisations,
Everyone*, spoke to us
kindly as though we were
a child, a single child.

The single child who'd done
the job of throwing
the message in the bottle
over the wire to where
*Journalists, Organisations,
Everyone* stood waiting

was one of *Everyone*.
Hello dear we adult everyones
might murmur through the fence
to her. She said it first though,
seemed to know it first
that everyone was dear.

IN THE TILTH

Inside the riddled ground
there must be ordinary
blind existence happening.
No light, no darkness, let
alone an anything
that glitters back especially
when a mole is flipping
through our soil with tooth-comb
fingers leaving little hills
of tilth. A gift for gardeners
as an only slightly rusted
ear-ring is for you,
long lost and handed back
into the upper air
as being unearthly.

RAINING UP

Rain then. Nothing much. The same
thin haze at the window
as these days you weep to yourself
when you come from nowhere
back up the stairs to a room
in someone else's house.

Then rain comes, the real
thing. Empties buckets
of black sky upside-down
on the rooftops, beats at
the window, beats at the river-bed
people call a street, can't not

bounce back into its own
downpour. Like someone's hope
closes its eyes, waiting
for nothing, even sleeps a little,
then wakes. Springs upwards in them
meeting their rain of tears.

CLIPS

Hatless, I take off my cycle-clips in awkward reverence.
from 'Church Going' by Philip Larkin

Cycle-clips come from another
world fast disappearing now
although we can't forget
that Larkin took off his
to go inside a church.
What's new is heart-clips.
These sound as though they're what
we have attached to us
when our poor hearts have over-
stretched themselves with feeling
and they need clipping back.
I've been sedated but I hope
heart surgeons, when they go
inside a heart, take off
their cycle-clips in awkward reverence.

BIKE RIDE

Glad we'd pumped our bikes up
when we set off to explore
an English forest you said
might be Darfur. No desert
but a stony track through trees
you said the Janjaweed had burnt
by now. They could come
any minute, still scorching
your people's land, still
killing off. You took us
skidding up side-paths,
through root-lined puddles
so our wheels whirled. You're
not avoiding. Up steep
uncyclable ways, every
revolution, every time
you force your pedals round,
you're even standing up to.

LONG SLOW FALL

Seems like this afternoon
not twenty years ago I
last fell off my bike.
It happened slowly, slowly
came to me my front wheel
was going somewhere else,
was jammed in one direction
while I went in the other.
Was gravity off duty
letting me think my thoughts
before I fell? It didn't flash,
my plan for a safe landing,
it lumbered through my head.
Would broken ribs be preferable
to a broken wrist? Once
you let your handlebars
go loose, might you save your arms,
crash-landing on your chest?
All this you're given time for
between what happens and
what's bound to happen after it.

JOINS

You bought a most tenacious
glue for me which says it's
perfect for a person
who wants to make their joins
invisible. It says the glue
dries crystal clear. Joins aren't
the same as joy of course
but sometimes very nearly:
knee-to-knee in bed or nose-
to-nose or looking at,
being looked at. I hope
the glue you bought won't take
even these fleeting joins
away with it. Why not
take the glue away, back
to the shop to tell them
crystal clear's no good, joins
are delightful even
surreptitious ones.

GREY GOLD

Some people seem to think
anything that's damaged,
cracked or torn or has
a hole in like our car
with one door held together
by a strip of parcel tape
should be made whole again,
complete, as good as new.

As good as new is too
good to be beautiful. This
parcel tape our car wears
aches like a war-wound
in the memory of a dry
stone wall in Cumbria
which jutted out too far
and into us. The tape

is grey, it sparkles
like the powdered gold
kintsugi-workers use
to make the cracks they mend
more beautiful. Maybe
we ought to sell our car
and say it's not quite new,
it's slightly better than.

SIR

You were Sir to me. Could
have been Peg Leg, the First
World War equipped you for it,
equipped your gruff affection
when one arm thrown round
our shoulders your tin leg
pushed out and took the ground
we stood on. Six foot four
you towered over nick-names,
easy chat, the lectern
in School Chapel. Once
you thanked the God
you worshipped (we did too
if worshipping was cowering
at your growl of words)
for swallows gathering
on wires, the glory of it.

CHILDREN CROSSING

A child's satchel carries quite
a weight of books and picnic
lunch to school although it goes
by car and anyway is nothing
next to what the children
bring back home across the river
wading over as it swirls down
off the mountain. It could
wash them off their feet.

Shoes in one hand, the shoulder
of the child in front of them
in the other, they cross as
all one serious body feeling
its way through water which can't
stop now it's felt a channel
for itself. As for education
they get home soaked in it,
come dripping learnedly in.

DOUBLE-ENDED SAW

in memory of Peter Rowe

Your father-in-law, you said,
vicarious father, vicar,
used a double-ended saw
for log-cutting when you stayed.
On ordinary days he kept
his sawing and next Sunday's
sermon to himself. But when
you came, he had a feast
in store, a to-and-fro
of thought proposed, responded to,
about religion, a to-and-fro
of pauses while the saw
continued cutting in its sleep
and you two worked at thinking.

Later most of us hung up
our saws except we went
on sawing, not slicing through
but going slightly deeper.

THE OTHER HALF

in memory of Catherine Scott

There's a photograph or half
a photograph of you at school
with half your Sixth Form
English Literature class
studying and not quite study-
ing a book. I haven't got
the other half which must join
on to this one and include
your closest friend who, I suppose,
is not quite studying either.
Has she sent a message?
In the photograph you're
looking up and in the process
of smiling back an answer.

DAWDLING

in memory of my late wife, Diana

You burst out once and said
I went too fast. Couldn't I
forget where we were going
and go slower, look at things?
Couldn't I dawdle sometimes
like you did? That was more
than twenty years ago since
when you've sped away from me
and I from you. I don't
think either of us thought
we'd go so far so quickly
from each other. Now that
the only being left to you
is being remembered, I want
to tell you I'm clinging to you,
going slowly, dawdling
as you race away through time.

THE SLOW MOVEMENT

Quite near us there's a gap
in the hedge between fields
where you used to go through a gate
and now there's wire. Yesterday
cows arrived, wanted, I guess,
the brilliant evening light.
They were darker than cream, almost honey.
How did they know my daughter
had phoned and I'd missed
my favourite part of one
of Schumann's Piano Quartets?
The slow movement it was.
A gap like that can be filled
if you don't mind seeing, not
hearing at all, what you missed,
the slow music of cows
at a gap in the hedge,
the honey of limbs when they move,
the flicking of tails.

BELIEVING IN EAGLES

Two buzzards in the blue
of the morning taking

the long way round and round
to the roof of the sky.

You can see the full span
of their wings held still

as they lean on the air
and it lifts them.

98% of eagles seen,
somebody told me,

are buzzards. These two
are the only buzzards

that are actually eagles.

RED KITE

in memory of Roger Champion

Wings flat, letting
the current carry, the kite
comes slowly over our house.

The sun's going down, the kite
must have sent its shadow across
the valley ahead of it.

Maybe it's home already
if home is the line of dark
green trees along the horizon.

They say your father's nearly
ready to go. He's dozing
flat out with his dying. Could

the breeze take him off too,
not far, to the heaven he's sent
his mind ahead to already, just

across the horizon from us?

FLOODS CAME

Floods came unwritten, un-
predicted. Something up
in the white of the mountains

must have been too much
for something. No rain,
no snow in the valleys,

only icy water swirling
down dry river-beds,
running over, filling

empty fields. Next morning
the sky is glittering
upwards from the earth,

the poem that you knew
you couldn't write
stares at you from its page.

SALVIA

Not cuckoo-spittle and not spat,
merely the dribble of saliva
older people sometimes aren't aware
has puddled between teeth and lips
and overflowed. This dribble
must have left its city when
floods made its teeming home
unliveable. First thing I know,
it's sliding down my chin. Is it too
much to hope disgust, disdain
slide down towards the heart
and into decency? What I wish
for these displaced, unwanted
is salvia, space on unflooded
earth to make a home and – is this
too much? – once the plants are sown,
for 'v' and 'i' to swap and salvia,
reds and blues, to spring up round it.

ARRANGEMENT WITH WATER

You have to learn to live with
our hot water system as
it does with you. This com-
plicity you have with it
is only needed in the mornings
when you want a shower.
You switch it on and hear it
in the distance coming so slowly
to its gargled coughed up
senses that you've time
to shave or make a cup of tea
and if you do this at the same
pace every day it will come
gushing out precisely when
you want it, at its own sweet will.

HALF-ARRANGING

I do like the way in which you fling words into the air...
– David Birmingham

At U.E.A. in Norwich
they fling, a whole Department
flings, their mortar-boards
into the air to celebrate
becoming graduates. Maybe
all students do the same,
watch them come floating down –
even hired mortar-boards
can float, can almost fly –
in half-arranged disorder
they'd never have imagined
if they hadn't flung.

WHY WOULD THE ROAD?

Why would the road from the village
slope down so steeply
if it didn't want you to follow,
free-wheeling if you have wheels?

And why would it then lead you
through a tunnel of green
so thick-knit you feel
your way through the night of it

if you didn't come through the trees
into the dazzle of ordinary,
clouds as clouds are I suppose
when no one's looking at them?

MOUNTAIN STREET

You might think Mountain Street
climbs up mountains maybe
over them. All it does is rise
and when it's risen to the point
it can't go further, it comes back.

Mountain Street's a street
that takes you through to nowhere.
Like most of us who live
on Mountain Street we can't
go further, we take our street's

example. We don't need mountains,
not when we pass the field
the geese return to every year.
They take what food there is, what
companionship, what ease.

SITTING BY ISLEDON ROAD

Scarcely a mile to walk
down Isledon Road from the Underground
at Finsbury Park and only
once a fortnight. Thank blind
goodness though for garden walls
along the way. Some of course
have railings set in concrete,
some are topped with jagged
tiles or glass but a few
are just the height, the angle
of a chair. One front garden
opposite the turning to Medina Rd.
always arrives exactly
when you need it. They're not
like street-lamps, regular,
these kind front garden walls.
They'll come but only when
you stop expecting them.
It isn't far, three bus-stops
at the most. In your right mind
and on your half-right legs
you wouldn't want to take the bus
and once a fortnight miss
the flat-topped garden walls
on Isledon Road.

PENCILLING OVER

I often used to ask
my mother for her help
with Maths though all she had
to do it with was love
and steady looking at.
As she looked her pencil
traced and re-traced words
I'd copied from the blackboard
and brought home from school.
Shame I haven't kept a copy
of her pencilling. Sometimes though
I find I'm following
the grooves where love or if
it's not the same thing steady
looking at had trailed its
pencil when my mother said
she'd help me with my Maths.

BALANCING ACT

It must be true, it's there
in black and white, a photograph
of Nolde's fifty years younger
second wife holding a cup
of tea up on her finger-
tips. Nolde and she are sitting
in his studio, paintings
like naughty children lined up
in front of them. Nolde
loved Germany, had high hopes
of Hitler. Hitler called
his art degenerate though,
even stopped him painting.
He looks inscrutably across
at her. Along the wall,
standing shoulder-to-shoulder,
almost joined, sea-spray,
huge rumbling skies, flowers.

AT THE ARTIST'S HOUSE

I wanted no one to see my pictures except a passer-by, someone who'd lost his way.
– Emil Nolde

I'm on my way to somewhere
if not sign-posted remembered
when I pass some paintings
in a garden perched in trees
or leaning on a house.
An old man at a window
sees me. 'Lost your way, have you?'
'No,' I say, 'I've been past here before.'
At which the old man stumbles
out and turns the paintings
round to face the wall. I think
he isn't angry, he's sorry
for me that I know too much,
I can't go artlessly through trees
and come upon a nowhere
I'm not looking for.

WAITING FOR WAYNE

Throughout the day a woman
in an office didn't say
but left a voice switched on
to say we needn't worry,
the engineer assigned to us
was still on schedule, every time
it rang was still on schedule.
And then when it was dark
Wayne phoned. We like Wayne,
not his fault he couldn't
get to us, he'd been delayed.
If only we had known, sometime
between 8 a.m. and 6, it was
Wayne who was on schedule,
Wayne who wasn't going to come.

IN GAS

My son's flatmate designed
a toughened workproof raincoat
for British Gas, North West.
Rugged as North West Gasmen,
their logo on my chest, I've worn
this raincoat for years. Gas
is nothing to me, mere talk,
though I have to admit
in crowds, in trains, in queues
people have smiled and said
they were in gas like me,
it was great, and I've said
'Wonderful, wasn't it?' back.

WEATHER AND NEWS

'Weather and news, Gertie,'
my grandfather called to his sister
on September 3rd just before
9 p.m.. Every evening
he would do the same
and we'd sit round in the last
of the light, in the almost
silent film of ourselves
on September 3rd, hearing
the news. I can't recall
a word the wireless said.
Someone must have told me
we were going to be fighting
a war and my great aunt
went gently round lighting
the gas on the walls. I
think there were little hisses
at first then each hiss
burst out into a flame.

IN THE QUEUE

Joined the queue for Maths.
The first of us to come would use
the hole our compasses had poked
in Tubby's classroom door.
Was our war-torn-open teacher
in a rage? Was the fragment
of the German shell which lodged
in Tubby's brain lying
peacefully or had it shelled
again? Sometimes our spy reported
Tubby was throwing chalk
at people's heads, sometimes
only words. Luckily for us,
though we were uniformed
already, we wouldn't be available
for fighting wars until Malaysia
or Korea (early 1950s).

PARALLEL LINES

After Japan surrendered in 1945 America and the Soviet Union decided to divide Korea along the line of the 38th parallel.

No food, no truth-telling, no light.
Wire, trenches, land-mines. After
school my brother went to fight
in the Korean War: entered
what's still impenetrable night.

Didn't get far, it seems. He might
have crossed the parallel. Maybe
he spent an infamous half-night
in 1953 being bombed alive
by the Chinese. No light.

He'd always told me things. One night
he'd let me know the facts of life
(some of them weren't quite right).
For years he kept what happened in Korea
in his own impenetrable night.

RAIN ON THE WINDOW

I thought the time was coming
when without announcement
one day we'd find the real
figures had been boarded up
too shameful to be known.
But the sky's still there,
the window that looks out at it
is unshuttered. There are
raindrops on it which I guess
are looking for a country
to be true in. Maybe
when you have power you don't
mind who knows what. You keep
the real figures unconcealed.
They're out there dribbling down
the far side of the window.

THE WISDOM OF ELI

It was Eli, my landlord's
handyman, who taught me to use
the broken shaft of a spade
to dig the holes for planting.
They seemed too cavernous
for slim green shoots. Just
drop them in, he said, and fill
the holes with water, nothing else.
Then let the darlings grow.

These darlings, these slim
green shoots, April, Catherine,
Sharif, Peter, Bridget, Ian
and now Roger, I want them all
to know by poem we've been
watching them stretch out
to the edges of the holes I dug,
now they can almost raise
themselves without our pain,

as we can almost without theirs.

FOR HAYMANOT

From where we are, which must be
fifty miles away, the flat land
that surrounds you is a desert.
No Nile flowing through it, no
green, no Ian to be with.

Sometime when you're ready
you'll hear water whispering
again, you'll see the land
spring back. When you're ready
maybe you'll want to plant.

Yes, in honour of, in loving
memory of. And in care for,
in affection for. Darkening
the soil at the root of.
Tending, letting be.

LIME-GRIEF

for Bridget Rowe

Lime-trees can't be faulted
in the way they grieve.

Deciduous and lofty
perhaps they find it easy

to forget the past, which
anyway took place modestly

a hundred feet below.
Lime-trees remind us though:

the honeydew that insects
suck from them in summer

oozes out and sticks
to surfaces it falls on,

on car-bonnets and on the thin
skin of our sense that we

were with you once, at ease,
at what seemed our best.

IN THE KITCHEN

The water for the washing up
came, comes still I think,
thanks to the heater on the wall,
which bursts out into breathy
action on demand. All
you do is turn the tap on
in the sink or stick
a scrap of paper on
the heater's smooth white surface
saying love you P and warmth
can't not unload itself
into a steaming bowl
where staining disappears
and cups smile white again
where lips have been.

LOVE NOTE

Charmer, uncrowned king
of refugees (I can't give
details, your region
of South London would be
overwhelmed with vehicles
parked illegally), you had
to wait for nine years
doing nothing till they saw
in modest you the perfect
Civil Enforcement Officer.
I can't say more except
we're setting off for somewhere
in South London where
we'll park illegally and hope
to find a Parking Notice
slipped like a love-note
in between our windscreen-
wipers and our windscreen.

HOW THE EYES SMILE

for Raga

Not caught in limelight
like celebrities. Not even when
a huge rejoicing sun
rises to your setting up
a charity for refugees
in South Sudan. This light
is different. It smiles
through your eyes. I think
it's when you're seeing
how things might be
and almost are since people
are so capable of loving.
This light comes on in you
with hoping for, believing.

SOMEWHERE BETWEEN

Somewhere between Laura Ingalls Wilder
and Nastase, the angry tennis star
whose pictures filled your walls, you
ran a business from your bedroom
selling dolls tucked up in beds
you made of walnut-shells.
Your business thrived. People phoned
with orders, a shop in Oxford
liked you. One day you even had
a customer booked in. 'Don't let him
see you, Dad, I want this man
to think I own the house.'
After he left I drove you into town
to buy you not quite regulation
nearly flat-heeled shoes for school.
Term started the next day.

SHUNT

Queen's Square we went to
when you, I guess, were 8.
Far too young, I realised,
when, stiffly vacant, sitting
on a bed, your doctor-grand-
father gazed through us
out beyond. Later something
called a shunt revived him
and he went home with his life.

I can't believe the hanging
open mind of your proud
grandfather could plant in you
the wish to be a doctor. Unless
in his vacancy he shunted on
to you his way of listening,
the way he heard a person
through, how he never knew
until he came to know.

DRILL

I'm pleased you chose
a drill this year to celebrate
your birthday. Not that I'm

fond of drills. Your mother though
would have been overjoyed
to give it to you and to see

you using it as safely,
as meticulously as she would
through a wall or door.

Such neat entrances
for you with your new drill
to follow her. I can't remember,

did we ever drill you?
Didn't we live alongside
and you couldn't not grow up?

ENID'S LADDER

The twist in the top of the ladder
my late wife's godmother
used for her pruning and picking
gets more pronounced with the years.
Two or three rungs from the top
the wood's so warped it seems
the neck of it jammed one day
when it was looking back to see
what lay behind it, the war
she fought from London, VE day,
the garden she made of old age.
No more looking forward.
At three rungs from the top
it's quite good to be warped, good
to discover what's been lying
behind the things you do. So much
to pick, so much to prune back.

BUTCHER'S NAME

I forget the name of the butcher
in the Oxford Covered Market
where we bought our weekend meat.
I remember the meat.
I remember how, playing
the organ at our church
on Sunday mornings, there
he was, our butcher, not
a trace of blood, I see,
smearing the keys. Even now
meat, Oxford, religion
spill out on each other as I carve them
clear of my life. No more
non-conformist hymns, no more punt-
poles stuck in Cherwell mud,
no more Lindsay's sausages.
There, I've remembered the name.

COLLISIONS

I still keep voices of small boats
especially of punts and rowing-boats
softly colliding with each other
in my head. These days collisions
happen much more angrily. It seems
our Threatforce wants a not
too public way of pushing boats
they don't approve of back
across the sea. I hope they don't
use poles like those we used to stir
up mud-clouds as we pushed
our lovers up and down the river
in a punt. These orange-jacketed
arrivers bring their own home
voices with them in their heads,
their soft collisions. A sloping beach
growls at them as they land.

HUMANITY

Seems the word humanity
has been deleted, can't be
used in argument any more.
Money we can handle,
count it up and say
how much it is. Human-
ity is not like that, it can't
mount up on money-changers'
tables, it doesn't when
the tables are upturned
go skidding off across the temple
floor. Humanity can still
be handcuffed though, blind-
folded, flown off to Rwanda.

HUMANS

for Mark Swain

We hadn't introduced you, you
had no means of knowing
who was who but as you queued
you noticed, so you said,
how gracious and attentive
the girl who had the job
of selling was to an old man
also queuing to buy a book.
The man could hardly stand, you said,
could hardly speak but she,
all eye-enchanting kindness,
fetched a seat and helped him
sit and choose a book, helped
him find the money in his wallet.
You didn't know these people.
Instead you made mankind of who
you saw, an old man smiling,
being smiled at by a girl.
You made womankind of her.

A THREAD OF COTTON

A thread of cotton with knots in it
that must have happened less
than half-way through her life
but kept on happening, hence
the pen and paper handed out.
Her friends had threads like her
with knots in them but loosely
tied, they didn't need to weep
untying them, unpicking thread
from thread, they soon slept nights
without a single knot. But then
a woman with a voice
she went on hearing told her
no knot is pulled so tightly
words can't worm themselves
inside and arch their backs
and leave your thread unknotted.

SURVIVOR

No rain now for weeks, not
much wind. The hollyhocks
stand tall, completely still, stiff
with surviving. A last flower
is a kiss that refuses
to be left unblown. Nothing
to say, too late now to leave
messages or meanings.

You have to flower in
the absence of yourself.
They ask you questions
but you don't know who
to look for looking for
a tall upstanding self.
In your empty stalk you know
the answers but you say
you can't remember and you can't.

NO TALKING BEFORE BREAKFAST

Love, I'm sorry but I like
our wordlessness when dozing
to go on unbroken until
almost breakfast-time. No
stories before 8 a.m., no quotes
from books you've woken to,
no dreams recounted. It's
words I'm thinking of.
Maybe we hear so harshly
in harsh morning light
words shrivel, lose their shape.
After 8 is fine. By then a word
has woken, is renewed, silvered
in the salt of dozing, stay-
ing under, swimming through
the swirl, the blur of it.
By then a word can speak.

ACEQUIA

(irrigation channel)

There's nothing much up there,
white mountain shouldering
the weight of deep blue sky
and water that's diverted
from its dark ravine
and chortles through the trees
in such an icy froth
you wouldn't need to worry
about words. They come out
washed and redefined
as smooth white stones the makers
centuries ago had paved
their ditches with to irrigate
the language and the land.

TOMATO-GROWING

We did all the right things,
grew our tomatoes in pots
in what might be a greenhouse,
fed them, watered them, strung them
to a ceiling which they grew
obediently up to. Maybe in
spite of, I suspect because of,
there's an unfed, unwatered,
unstrung, not even planted
heap of tomato surging
up through flowers twenty yards
away outside. Its fruit is plent-
iful, it clusters, pulls down bran-
ches, jostles to be praised.
Earth-crusted, rough to touch, no
good for supermarkets, it's grown
itself without us even knowing.

MAN OUTSIDE

Receipt UGK4
records the fact that man
outside received a cup
of coffee called Americano
on 29th September 2022
at 11.49. Man outside
drank the coffee, thanked
woman inside for coming out
to serve him. These days
man quite liked being man
outside, he'd learnt to let
worms rise, tomatoes redden,
and the breath he thought he breathed
breathe him breathe him breathe him
while he sat outside it
drinking coffee called Americano.

BEDTIME STORY

In the long wait for your tea
Submarines, a short history
is what, aged 4, you choose
for me to read to you.
You know it all already,
especially that when the sea
is frozen submarines
can go along beneath it
and come up icebergs later.
You close your eyes as you go
gently under. When you wake
you have to crack an ice-field
open to come back. "Is it
still today?" you ask.

HOSPITAL

We are lucky, we have a window
in our ward. We can't see sky
only the next bit of hospital
much taller than our bit.
We can't see in, what
we stare up at is metal
beams, bars, girders, funnels
painted warship-grey, bolted
together at right angles.
They work late up there.
It's our early hours
when they switch off.
I think there is nobody there
but scaffolding. They don't have
patients like we do. Only
hospital, bits bolted together
at all the right angles.

MOON POEM

You'll be at the bedroom-window now
marvelling. You've always loved
the moon. Back here in hospital

a pillow I keep on a ledge
at the top of the bed, next
to my head, drops lightly onto me.

Being in hospital's a marvel
when you rest your hand
on my shoulder like that.

WORMING IN

One of Mr Sunak's tasks has been to conceal the rift between
the two wings of his party.

How to worm apart
the sealing, the re-sealing
of air-proof packages?
I can unscrew a bottle top,
sometimes wrench loose the lid
of a container, but my breakfast
prunes this morning I could
only look at lurking
inside their bag. How
to rip open difference
when two sides, two unsmiling
opponents cling to each other
with no way between? No chance
with the shower gel this morning.
Even my breakfast-knife
couldn't stab a way through.

A AND E

There's a girder I recognise
just outside the window
of my current ward. Riddled
with little bolting-holes
you can see where we got
bolted in ourselves. All
we can do is wait. Even
being patient leaves its mark,
girders us around, dangles
the shape of itself out-
side our minds until
we can't help recognising
how we came to A and E
and endless patience is what
they've bolted into us.

UNFIXED ABODE

I'm wrenching open or I'm
not quite wrenching open
the lid of something I used
to spin round and it spun,
it's grooves were perfect not stuck
on grindings of old jam.

I'm always wrenching, spinning,
always being spun the way
in hospital they tell you
you're moving wards again
in half an hour and whirl
you through the corridors and lifts
still in your bed. This must be
my seventh in seven weeks.

NO FEAR

I remember thinking, now
there's nothing to fear.
That was twenty years ago,
it's out of date. The man
in the bed next to me
shouts at night for his sons.
I haven't said it but I've
told him all he can do
is murmur the names or think them.
Out of date is when you drift
into a different reach
of being, of no date at all,
no remembering, no shouting
through a night impenetrable
as this. Nothing left to fear.